CCSS **Genre** Folktale

MW00908634

Essential Question
What makes different animals unique?

The Ballgame
Between the Birds
and the Animals

A Cherokee Folktale

retold by Anna Fenton • illustrated by Sarah Snow

Chapter 1
The Challenge

One day, the four-legged animals challenged the birds to a ballgame. The birds agreed, and they all **gathered** in the meadow.

There were two poles. The animals painted their pole with bright colors. The birds put **fabulous** feathers on their pole. Each team had to stop the other team and hit its own pole with the ball. The first team to do this would win the game.

STOP AND CHECK

How would the game be won?

The bear was captain of the animals.
"I can push things out of my way,"
he roared.

The turtle said, "My shell is hard.
Nothing can hurt me."

"I am faster than the birds," the
deer said.

The eagle was captain of the birds. The birds were brave, but they still felt afraid. The animals were so big and strong! The animals were **boasting** that they would win.

STOP AND CHECK

Why did the animals think they could win?

Chapter 2
New Teammates

The game was about to begin. Then two **creatures** appeared. They climbed up a tree by the **watchful** eagle.

"We want to play," they said. "Can we be on your team?"

"You both have four legs," said the eagle. "You belong on the animal team."

"We **offered** our help. But the animals laughed at us," said the first creature.

"We are so small," said the second one.

The eagle felt sorry for the creatures. "You can be on our team," he said.

Then the hawk said, "These creatures have no wings! They can't be on the bird team."

The birds thought about this. Then they had an idea. The birds got a leather drum. They took the leather off the drum. They cut out two wings from the leather. They **stretched** the wings as far as they could. Then they put them on one of the creatures. This is how the bat came to be.

STOP AND CHECK

Why didn't the hawk want the creatures to be on the birds' team?

There was no leather to make wings for the second creature. The eagle and the hawk used their beaks. They pulled at the second creature's skin. They stretched out the sides of its body. This is how the flying squirrel came to be.

The birds were pleased. They had a very good bird team.

STOP AND CHECK

How were the bat and the flying squirrel created?

Chapter 3

Game Time!

At last, the **signal** was given, and the game began. The flying squirrel grabbed the ball. He carried it into a tree.

The animals couldn't reach the ball.
When it fell, the deer ran after it.
But the swallow got the ball and tossed
it to the bat.

The bat **swooped** low. The bear **lumbered** toward the bat to catch him, but the bat zipped quickly past. He hit the ball against the feather pole.

The animals stood there in **disbelief**. The birds had won the game! It was a **splendid** day for the birds.

How did the birds win the game?

15

Respond to Reading

Summarize

Summarize what was special about the animals in this story. Use the chart to help you.

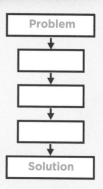

Text Evidence

1. What problem did the first creature have? How was it solved?

   Problem and Solution

2. Find the word *zipped* on page 14. What does it mean? What clues helped you figure it out? Vocabulary

3. Write about the second creature's problem. How did the birds solve the problem? Write About Reading

Compare Texts
Read about what makes bats unique.

All About Bats

Bats are **unique**. They are the only mammals that can fly. Mammals have fur or hair. These animals feed milk to their babies.

There are many kinds of bats. One is as small as a bee.

The bumblebee bat is the smallest bat in the world.

17

Bats have special **features**. They can fly in the dark. But they don't crash into things. Bats can do this because they make squeaking

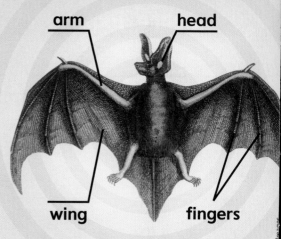

arm head

wing fingers

sounds. The sounds hit things. The sounds come back like echoes. The echoes help bats find safe paths.

Bats can find their way in the dark.

Vampire bats are small. Many people are afraid of them. But vampire bats don't usually harm people.

Vampire bats drink blood from cows and birds. Vampire bats take only a little blood each night. They make small cuts, so the animals aren't hurt.

Make Connections

How does *All About Bats* tell you what makes this animal unique? Essential Question

What kinds of animals are the creatures in *The Ballgame Between the Birds and the Animals*? Text to Text

Focus on
Genre

Folktales A folktale is a story that is passed down over time. Some things in folktales can't happen in real life. Some folktales teach a lesson.

Read and Find *The Ballgame Between the Birds and the Animals* is a folktale. Birds did not create bats and flying squirrels. The lesson is that kindness and clever thinking can be rewarded.

Your Turn

Write your own folktale. This can be your version of an old folktale, or it can be a new folktale.